BUILDING GODLY CHARACTER

by Ray Bentley

THE WORD
FOR TODAY
PO Box 8000, Costa Mesa, CA 92628

Building Godly Character
by Ray Bentley
General Editor: Chuck Smith

Published by **The Word For Today**
P.O. Box 8000, Costa Mesa, CA 92628
(800) 272-WORD (9673)
http://www.twft.com

© 1995, 2002 The Word For Today
ISBN 0-936728-59-9

Table of Contents

Preface.. i

Introduction.. iii

Chapter I..1

The Heart of a Shepherd.............................1

Laying the Foundation 1

Lessons in the Fields....................................3

The Way, the Truth, the Life 9

Chapter II 11

Facing Giants, Glorifying God..................11

The Anointing of the Lord 13

In the Name of the Lord 15

Facing the Giant..17

The Lesson of Goliath.................................20

Chapter III..23

The People God Uses 23

Samuel, Man of Prayer 24

Saul, the Iron 26

Jonathan, Beloved Friend...........................28

Chapter IV...33

Lessons From the Cave 33

A Rising Star...33

An Angry King...34

Dark Days 35
So Now What? 37

Chapter V 47
Halftime 47
One Step From Eternity 47
Success to Significance 51
A Foundation of Grace 55

Chapter VI 57
No Compromise 57
David's Epitaph 57
Restoring a Compromised Nation 59
"I never knew you..." 61
How to Return to the Kingdom of God 63

Chapter VII 67
A Man After God's Own Heart 67
A Disappointing Setback 68
Sin 69
Nathan, the bravest man in the kingdom 71
Confession Time 73
Grace 74
Character 76
In closing… 78
How to Become a Christian 79

Preface

When Luke wrote the message of the gospel to Theophilus, he declared that his desire was to set forth in order a declaration of those things that are most surely believed among us. Luke desired that Theophilus might know the certainty of those things in which he had been instructed.

We seem to be living in a day of spiritual confusion. Paul wrote to the Ephesians that they not be as children tossed to and fro with every wind of doctrine by the slight of men and the cunning craftiness whereby they lie in wait to deceive. Because of all the confusion in the church today, and the many winds of doctrine that continue to blow through the body of Christ, we felt that it would be good to have various pastors write booklets that would address the issues and give to you the solid biblical basis of what we believe and why we believe it.

Our purpose is that the spiritual house that you build will be set upon the solid foundation of the eternal Word of God, thus we know that it can withstand the fiercest storms.

Pastor Chuck Smith
Calvary Chapel of Costa Mesa, California

Introduction

When God calls us to follow and serve Him, He also begins the process of building our character.

After the Lord told Samuel to anoint David as King over Israel, ten to fifteen years passed before David was allowed to take the throne. In the meantime, God was building his character.

Right after Jesus met Paul on the road to Damascus, the Lord revealed that Paul was His chosen vessel to carry the Gospel to the Gentiles. But ten years passed before Paul went on his first missionary journey. During that time, God was building his character.

When God chose Moses to lead the children of Israel out of bondage, He allowed circumstances that put Moses in the wilderness for forty years. Forty years of character building!

We cannot bypass character development. "Being confident of this very thing, that He who has begun a good work in you will complete it until the day of Jesus Christ," is what Paul wrote to the Philippians (1:6). When God calls us to Him, He begins a work in us that will cause us to love Him, and consequently, to long to know Him, follow Him and serve Him.

In the process, He conforms us into the image of His Son (Romans 8:29). He transforms us by renewing our minds (Romans 12:2). He takes a new creation (2 Corinthians 5:17), and molds us into a vessel which can be used for His glory (2 Timothy 2:21).

God wants us to be people whose strengths and capabilities come from Him. He wants us to be people who acknowledge that it is "in Him we live and move and have our being" (Acts 17:28). This is what character building is all about.

Sometimes the process is difficult, lengthy, puzzling, even painful. As we shall see through Scriptural example, it is necessary. The quality, depth and strength of our character is a reflection of our relationship with the Lord. And nothing else in our lives matters more.

The word *character* comes from a root word which means "to tear, cut in, engrave, cut into furrows." Character is formed through an engraving process, a process of having something cut into and indelibly marked into something else. In our lives, it is the experiences which are literally engraved into our souls which build our personalities, and influence our convictions, our desires, our actions—our character.

But this is not all left up to chance. In His sovereignty, God orders all the steps of our lives. He never promised us smooth traveling. He allows bumps and twists and turns in the road—even a few dangerous pits. Through these circumstances, He teaches us, molds us, and most importantly, causes us to be more dependent upon Him.

With each new experience, another stroke of the Master's chisel is engraved upon our souls, shaping us into the image of His Son, building in us the character God desires in His people.

While there are numerous character building examples in Scripture, few are as detailed, dramatic and applicable to our own lives as King David's life. I believe the formation of David's character gives us a clear and true picture of how God goes about dealing with each one of us.

CHAPTER I

THE HEART OF A SHEPHERD

"He will feed His flock like a shepherd; He will gather the lambs in His arm, and carry them in His bosom, and gently lead those who are with young."

Isaiah 40:11

Laying the Foundation

"He chose us in Him before the foundation of the world..."

(Ephesians 1:4)

God chooses whom He will use. Sometimes the choice seems unlikely—even absurd. This is the beginning of character building. God chooses to use us in a situation to which we seem unsuited—and He goes about the process of preparing us.

Look at how He chose David to be king over Israel.

To begin with, David was not the people's first choice. In complete rebellion against God's plan for the nation, the people demanded a king "like all the other nations." They were kids who wanted to be like everyone else! So they got their king, Saul, and he was everything they wanted and expected him to be.

Saul was a movie star king. He fit the part perfectly in outward appearance. "There was not a more handsome person than he among the children of Israel. From his shoulders upward he was taller than any of the people," we read in 1 Samuel 9:2. He came from a respected family, had a good reputation and was wealthy besides.

Saul epitomized the best of human achievement. Besides his looks and background, he had proven himself brave, heroic, enthusiastic and generous. But there was a small glitch—he was consumed with himself. His prideful and jealous nature eventually hardened his heart, causing him to turn away from God's Spirit.

Saul's problems began, but not because he had human frailties. Those are the very things God works through in our lives, when we allow His Spirit free reign. No, it was pride that destroyed Saul. Pride caused him to ignore the prophet Samuel's counsel, to turn against his own son, Jonathan, and those who loved him, and ultimately to rebel against the Lord. In spite of his natural abilities, his kingdom was soon in trouble.

Lessons in the Fields

Meanwhile, out in the fields of Judea a young boy of perhaps 16 was being prepared to take Saul's place.

The Lord sent His prophet Samuel to the house of Jesse, in Bethlehem, where He assured the old prophet that a king would be found.

One by one, Jesse paraded seven fine looking sons before Samuel. One or two of them looked like such good candidates that Samuel thought to himself, "Surely the Lord's anointed is before Him."

But as each one passed before Samuel, the Lord said *No*, reminding the prophet, "The Lord does not see as man sees; for man looks at the outward appearance, but the Lord looks at the heart."

Finally, Samuel asked, somewhat exasperated, "Are all the young men here?"

Jesse responded, "There remains yet the youngest, and there he is, keeping the sheep" (1 Samuel 16:11). Jesse almost ignored this youngest son, David. He just seemed too young, and after all, he was merely a shepherd boy, not a soldier like his brothers. But as soon as David was brought in, the Lord spoke to Samuel, "Arise, anoint him; for this is the one!"

This must have shocked Jesse. He had so little respect for his youngest son that he didn't even bother to call him in from the fields. But David was right where God wanted him. His youth and occupation made him an unlikely candidate for king, but from God's perspective, he was learning exactly what he would need for the future.

Later in his life David wrote in the twenty-third Psalm, "The Lord is my shepherd." He wrote from personal knowledge. As a young man, David not only learned to trust the Lord as his shepherd, but he learned some very specific lessons while he was being prepared to become a shepherd to God's people.

Loneliness

David understood loneliness because he spent so many hours out in the fields, with no company but the sheep entrusted to his care. Many great leaders testify to the loneliness of their positions. It would be nearly impossible to lead a nation if you were not prepared for the times when you will stand alone; the times when you will have to make a hard decision or need to shepherd your people through difficult situations.

It was here, sitting under the stars at night and the hot sun during the day, that David's spiritual life began to mature. He diligently watched over his flock, but he also allowed his mind and heart to stretch beyond the confines of the fields before him. We know from the Psalms he wrote that he began in his youth to contemplate the mysteries of the Lord.

"My voice You shall hear in the morning, O Lord," he sang in Psalm 5. How often he must have spent those early hours as the sun began to peek over the hills, calling upon the name of the Lord. There was no one else around, so he learned to communicate with God and God alone.

"In Your presence is fullness of joy," he would write later (Psalm 16:11). David learned that even in his loneliest moments, his Good Shepherd would be near, drawing him into His loving presence.

Loneliness would become an issue many times in the years to come, but David had learned through loneliness the awareness of God's presence.

Listening to God

"When I consider the heavens," David wrote, "the work of Your fingers, the moon and the stars, which You have ordained, what is man that You are mindful of him?" (Psalm 8:3,4).

He also looked up at the skies and around him at the beauty of the earth and exclaimed, "The heavens declare the glory of God; and the firmament shows His handiwork. Day unto day utters speech, and night unto night reveals knowledge" (Psalm 19:1,2).

David recognized that God speaks through His creation. Over and over we read in the Psalms a passion for the glory of God's creation.

In his book *A Shepherd Looks at the Twenty-third Psalm*, Phillip Keller, himself a shepherd, recalls, "Looking up at the star-studded sky I remember that at least 250,000,000 x 250,000,000 such bodies...have been scattered across the vast spaces of the universe by His hand...All this is but humbling. It drains the 'ego' from a man and puts things in proper perspective."

David had learned respect and awe for God's creation, and as a result, his life was in "proper **perspective**." He knew who he was in relation to the **power** of God manifested through His creation. He recognized the awesome design and **order** of the universe which God had ordained and set into motion.

No wonder he asked, "Who is man that You are mindful of him?"

David listened to God through His creation, and understood the awesome magnificence of his Lord.

Love for the Sheep

Sheep depend greatly on their shepherd. The same holds true of a nation. God wanted a leader for His people who would love them as well as lead and guide them. Therefore, He chose a shepherd.

Sheep need a lot of care and for the most part they are defenseless creatures. Just like us. God was forming the character of Christ in David, and there was no better place to start than tending sheep. Shepherding tends to give one a love for defenseless creatures.

"I am the good shepherd," Jesus said. "The good shepherd gives His life for the sheep" (John 10:11). He used Himself as an example of a shepherd and the act of laying down His life as the example of how one should love the sheep. When Jesus looked upon the multitudes of people, "He was moved with compassion for them, because they were weary and scattered, like sheep having no shepherd" (Matthew 9:36). This is the heart David would need one day for the nation of Israel.

We know from David's own account in 1 Samuel 17 that more than once he risked his life, fighting off wild beasts, to save his sheep.

Think about this for a second. Most teenagers, when faced with a lion walking off with a lamb in its ferocious jaws, would back off and say, "Hey, enjoy lunch." I know I probably would have. After all, it's just one little lamb.

But not David. He had too much love and respect for his father. He wasn't about to lose even one of his father's sheep.

This is exactly what God was looking for: a man who would love and lead his Heavenly Father's sheep, one at a time. David learned his lesson well. He would fight for his flock, as well as tend to their everyday needs, with a loving and compassionate heart.

The Way, the Truth, the Life

It is no accident that the day God called upon Samuel to anoint David king of Israel, David was found tending the sheep.

Those who believe they are called to be leaders, can take note of this. Pastoring, leadership and ministry is about tending and feeding the sheep. If we are not willing to be faithful in the seemingly small and "lowly" tasks of taking care of God's people, we will never be trusted with more.

God recently impressed upon me the simple yet powerful truth of Jesus' statement in John 14:6: "I am the way, the truth and the life."

How do we implement this into our lives and ministries? By following the example of a shepherd and his sheep.

Sheep need to follow their shepherd. They need to be fed by the shepherd. The only way they will have life, is to fulfill the shepherd's plan. Sheep won't live if they don't have a shepherd.

So, going back to John 14:6, as believers in Jesus Christ, I believe that we are supposed to be:

Following Jesus;
  He is the only **way**

Feeding on God's Word;
  He is the only **truth**

Fulfilling God's purposes for our lives;
  only then will we have eternal and
  abundant **life.**

When we follow our Good Shepherd, He will lead us to green pastures and still waters, restore our souls and keep our lives in His care (Psalm 23). This is what the Lord has always wanted for His people.

God had a specific purpose for calling a young and politically inexperienced shepherd boy out of the fields one day to anoint him king over Israel.

But fifteen more years had to pass before David could ascend the throne. God had more character building to do.

CHAPTER II

FACING GIANTS, GLORIFYING GOD

"Rejoice, O young man, in your youth..."

Ecclesiastes 11:9

"I will praise thee, O Lord my God, with all my heart: and I will glorify thy name for evermore."

Psalm 86:12

Recently, tennis champion Boris Becker was interviewed during Wimbledon. He commented that he wished he had the attitude at age 27 that he had at age 17—an attitude that says, "I can't lose!" Shortly afterward, he went to the court and defeated Andre Agassi. Perhaps recapturing his youthful boldness is what did it.

You have to wonder what David was thinking the day he faced Goliath. He was so young and full of faith! He couldn't lose. But I think he was fueled by more than a desire to win a battle. He had another cause in his heart. Look at what he said when he first heard the men of Israel discussing Goliath, the giant champion of the dreaded Philistines: "Who is this uncircumcised Philistine, that he should defy the armies of the living God?" (1 Samuel 17:26).

David was indignant! "How dare he defy the honor of God!" The seasoned warriors around him must have looked at him with some amusement and amazement. His own brother, treating him like the kid that he was, became angry with him. "What are you doing here anyway? Go home and tend your sheep."

But David was fired up. "Let no man's heart fail him," he pledged to the king. "I'll go fight the Philistine."

The Anointing of the Lord

What gave David so much passion at such a tender age? What gave him the courage to take on such a dangerous mission?

I believe the answer lies in the events that took place the day Samuel visited Jesse's house.

Did David understand what had just happened to him? "The Spirit of the Lord came upon David from that day forward," is what the Scriptures say of the moment Samuel anointed him king. *The Spirit of the Lord came upon David.* That explains everything.

Up until now, David had been a boy, learning patience and the ways of the Lord by tending his father's sheep. Soon after his anointing, he is described as, "skillful in playing, a mighty man of valor, a man of war, prudent in speech and a handsome person; and the Lord is with him" (1 Samuel 16:18).

David's status had risen considerably in a short time! Even if he wasn't fully aware of what was going on, the Holy Spirit was with him to such a degree that others recognized a change in him. He had been personally chosen by God, anointed with His Spirit, and was being transformed by the power of the Spirit into a man after God's own heart. He had been given a purpose and a calling upon his life. He was literally inspired to serve and honor the Lord.

What I *don't* see here is evidence of political ambition in David. At this point in his life, he was responding first to the Holy Spirit and secondly, to his training as a shepherd.

Besides learning to tend sheep, David gained two valuable skills in his father's field: he learned to play the harp, and he became skilled and courageous in defending his flock against wild beasts.

His musical ability brought him to the king's court: "David would take a harp and play it with his hand. Then Saul would become refreshed and well, and the distressing spirit would depart from him" (1 Samuel 16:23). He was learning how to minister with compassion, as well as being drawn into the inner workings of the court.

When the armies of the Philistines began to mobilize against Israel, championed by Goliath, David could observe Saul's reaction: dismay and fear. The king was out of fellowship with the Lord. He had no resources or strengths from which to draw.

No one else knew what to do either. The nation was floundering, like a flock of scared sheep, lacking a strong shepherd. They were about to be devoured by wild men. They needed a defender. David had been trained for the job.

The lowly shepherd boy, and the king's musician was about to become a national hero.

In the Name of the Lord

David stepped up to the challenge, I believe, with an uppermost purpose in mind. "How dare he defy the honor of God?" he cried. He was angered by the Philistine's brazen defiance.

David faced an enemy who was clothed and equipped with the finest the world had to offer: a bronze helmet, a coat of arms, weapons—all the best. David had no time for strategy meetings or for getting outfitted in suitable armor. He had no weapons but a slingshot and five stones.

Even so, look at what he said to Goliath: "You come to me with a sword, with a spear, and with a javelin. But I come to you in the name of the Lord of hosts, the God of the armies of Israel, whom you have defied" (17:45).

He was about to have every dangerous weapon available to his enemy thrown at him! And how does he respond? *"I come to you in the name of the Lord..."*

There are days when I think there are fiery darts, javelins, spears—everything in the enemy's arsenal—whizzing by my head. Do you ever feel that way? Swords are drawn to dissect us. Darts piercing our hearts. Defeat is imminent. We're powerless. We're facing giants.

Then we react the way Saul did— with fear and dismay. I have a feeling Goliath didn't look so big to David. David's faith was bigger than a giant. David was determined to defend the honor of God and had no time for fear.

David had a passionate desire to glorify God. That passion is what gave David his strength, his ability and ultimately his place in history. It gave him the ability to call upon the Lord with complete confidence.

Where did this passion come from? Remember, when Samuel anointed David, the Scripture says, "the Spirit of the Lord came upon David." What happened to David was explained years later by John the Baptist.

Talking about the Lord, John told his followers, "I indeed baptize you with water...but He will baptize you with the Holy Spirit and fire" (Matthew 3:11). The day David was anointed, the Holy Spirit was poured out upon him; a flame was kindled in his soul, a flame that could not be quenched, even by a godless bully.

Facing the Giant

Remember, David was still young—probably a teenager, maybe in his early twenties. He had just left home. From the security of a large family and daily responsibilities, he had been summoned to the king's court.

His diligence and faithfulness had been proven in his daily work. He had been true to the principle later set down in Zechariah 4:10: "Who has despised the day of small things?" He had been faithful in daily, small tasks.

This reminds me of the early days of the Calvary Chapel movement when many of the first pastors studying under Chuck Smith learned the work of the ministry through the "small" things—janitorial work, scrubbing toilets, ushering, taking care of children, tending to the needs of those living in the House of Psalms and Mansion Messiah, the Christian houses set up by Calvary Chapel. Everyone, like David, was young, excited about the Lord, caught up in a great work of the Holy Spirit and ready to turn the world upside down!

Now David, with all his youthful courage, his faith, his fervency and bravado, was ready to face the giant: "This day the Lord will deliver you into my hand," he called to Goliath. "I will strike you and take your head from you. And this day I will give the carcasses of the camp of the Philistines to the birds of the air and the wild beasts of the earth, that all the world may know that there is a God in Israel."

Whew!

In that one courageous act, David established his desire to live a life glorifying to God. Not that he would always succeed. David would have his times of strength, his moments of weakness; his times of victory, his days of defeat. But throughout his life, his desire to serve the Lord, his passion for knowing God, his heartbroken repentance when he sinned, never left him. In his darkest hours, he was able to seek the glory of the Lord. You can read it in his Psalms.

David faced another giant of a different sort in the twilight of his years. The giant was David's own sin. Even as he faced this giant, his enduring desire to honor the Lord is evident.

David had taken a census of the land, numbering the people, in disobedience to the Lord. As soon as it was done, he knew he had sinned.

Look at David's reaction: "I have sinned in what I have done; but now I pray, O Lord, take away the iniquity of your servant" (2 Samuel

24:10). Right away he repented and turned to the Lord.

The Lord offered David three choices: seven months of famine, three months of being pursued by enemies, or three days of plague.

"Please let us fall into the hand of the Lord, for His mercies are great" (24:14), was David's response. Such was David's relationship with the Lord, that even in his guilt and sin, he was willing to trust in the love and mercy of God. David knew God's heart intimately.

The Lord sent the plague, striking down thousands of people. When an angel of the Lord was sent to stop the destruction, the angel was found by the threshing floor of Araunah, the Jebusite.

The story ends with David buying the threshing floor from Araunah, to build an altar. Discovering the king's intentions, Araunah bowed down before David and offered to give his threshing floor and oxen and whatever was needed for a proper sacrifice.

David responded, "No, but I will surely buy it from you for a price; nor will I offer burnt offerings to the Lord my God with that which costs me nothing."

Once again, David wanted to give his all for the Lord. He did not take the easy way. *He would not give to God "that which costs me nothing."*

David bought the site and erected an altar to worship the Lord. This is the very site on which Solomon built the great Temple. God chose this same mountain as the place where His Son, Jesus Christ, would be crucified years later. David had truly established this place as a site where God would be glorified.

The Lesson of Goliath

As a young man, David fought the giant and won. Whether he would have had the same kind of courage in later years, we don't know. We certainly see evidence of bravery and heroism, but we also see times of weakness, even cowardice.

But David never lost his desire to live a life glorifying to God. When he sinned, he repented. When he was confused or weak, he turned to the Lord:

"For You are my lamp, O Lord;

the Lord shall enlighten my darkness.

For by You I can run against a troop;

By my God I can leap over a wall"

(2 Samuel 22:29-30).

Once again, the Lord was building godly character into David through all of his experiences. Jesus said many years later, "I have glorified You on the earth. I have finished the work which You have given Me to do" (John 17:4). David's desire to live his life in the same manner was a foreshadowing of the Messiah.

I can imagine David in his later years, perhaps when he was dealing with doubts and wondering if he had done right by the Lord he loved so much, remembering that day of victory against Goliath. I don't believe he ever doubted where the strength to defeat Goliath came from, or to Whom the glory should be given. He knew it was all the Lord.

With a memory like that to stir his soul, no wonder he remained throughout his days a man after God's own heart.

CHAPTER III

THE PEOPLE GOD USES

"As iron sharpens iron, so a man sharpens the countenance of his friend."

Proverbs 27:17

Often the tools of God's engraving process, as He writes the character of His Son into our hearts, come in the form of other people. And what sharp tools they can be!

Like all of us, David had people in his life, especially in those early years, who were instrumental in developing his character. We can all look back and remember certain individuals—parents, friends, teachers, neighbors— who either blessed us or brought heartache and turmoil into our lives. Either way, they were part of God's plan for our lives.

Since Romans 8:28 is one of God's promises—"And we know that all things work together for good to those who love God and are called according to his purpose"— then "all things" must include the people who cross our paths.

Samuel, Saul and Jonathan each played a different role in David's life. In each case, it was a role that fit perfectly into God's plan for David. As you read about them, take the time to think about people in your life. Perhaps learning how God used these three men in David's life will give you some insight as to how God is using certain people in your own life.

Samuel, Man of Prayer

Everyone needs a Samuel in their lives: An older, wiser person, filled with the Spirit, anointed in following God's leading and able to see something in you that no one else can quite fathom. Samuel listened to the Lord and knew David was the chosen king, even though his youth and circumstances said otherwise. Samuel was a man of prayer; because of his prayer life, his discernment and wisdom could be trusted.

When I think of Samuel, I think of Pastor Chuck Smith. In the early days of Calvary Chapel, I believe the Lord gave him special discernment. He was able to see God's hand in the lives of many young men and women whom others were ready to write off as unredeemable. Or, if they were saved, they certainly weren't fit to be in the ministry.

Pastor Chuck laid hands on and anointed many young pastors who had come out of the hippie and drug scene, who were spiritually young, but like David, full of love for the Lord and zeal to serve. He saw the Spirit of the Lord at work, even if few others did.

As a result, many of those who learned under Pastor Chuck went on to be pastors, teachers, evangelists, missionaries and all manner of servants of the Lord. Many of those ministries have gone on to bear an abundance of fruit for the Kingdom of God—and to spill into the next generation.

God uses the Samuels in the church to pray for, encourage and build the characters of future servants of the Lord.

When no one else could imagine David as king, Samuel listened to the Lord and anointed

him. Only Samuel knew that this was God's
chosen king.

Saul, the Iron

Whether we want to admit it or not, we
probably all need a Saul in our lives. Without
Saul, David could not have become the king that
he was.

Saul was alternately a friend and an
enemy—more often an enemy. He was driven
by jealousy and insecurity. Spiritually, he was in
constant turmoil because he resisted the Lord.
He made David's life miserable! Because of Saul,
David became a fugitive, running for his life. He
was forced to live by his faith and his wits.
Exiled into the wilderness, he hid and lived in
dark caves. He learned to cope with fear, failure,
depression, betrayal—and whether he realized it
or not, God used all of it to shape and build his
character.

It is never pleasant to have a Saul in one's
life. But it is most likely necessary if we are to
learn certain lessons, such as:

The power of prayer in dealing with hard
circumstances. David prayed often, sometimes
brutally, about Saul and those who persecuted
him. Read the Psalms. They're full of his prayers
for deliverance. "O, God, deliver me! Let them
be ashamed and confounded who seek my life;

Let them be confused...who desire my hurt" (Psalm 70:1-2). He learned to rely on prayer as his source of strength. God often allows us to be put in circumstances where we have no choice but to pray. He wants us to come to Him with our needs.

The sovereignty of God. In spite of people who appear to be roadblocks in your life, who wrongfully accuse you, persecute you, or work against you, God is greater and will keep you in His care. As you continue to seek Him, you'll see how He will orchestrate the events of your life according to His will.

"Now I know that the Lord saves His anointed," David wrote (Psalm 20). "Forever, O Lord, Your word is settled in heaven" (Psalm 119:89). The plan God had for David's life could not be thwarted by Saul's tortured life.

Honor in the face of persecution. David had been mercilessly persecuted by Saul. He had every right to retaliate, by the law of the land, and he was recognized by most of the people as the rightful king. But one day, when he discovered Saul alone and unguarded in a cave, vulnerable to attack, David resisted his own impulses and the urging of his companions. "The Lord forbid that I should do this thing to...the Lord's anointed....

So David restrained his servants with these words" (1 Samuel 24:6-7).

David's character was severely tested through his relationship with Saul, but the lessons he learned would serve him well when he became king. No one sharpened David's character more than Saul.

Jonathan, Beloved Friend

If we are truly fortunate, we will be blessed with a Jonathan in our lives. In his book "Twelve Things I Want My Kids To Remember," Jerry Jenkins writes, "Cultivate at least one life-long friend. The media pretends that such relationships are common. Ask around. You'll discover they're rare. And priceless." Jonathan was that rare and priceless friend to David.

If a Saul sharpens your life, makes you a little wiser, wary, and shrewder, a Jonathan brings balance through love, commitment, loyalty and trust. A Jonathan can be a trusted friend, brother, sister or spouse. In David's case, he was the son of his worst enemy.

We read in 1 Samuel 18, "the soul of Jonathan was knit to the soul of David, and Jonathan loved him as his own soul...then Jonathan and David made a covenant... And Jonathan took off the robe that was on him and gave it to David, with his armor, even to the sword and his bow and his belt."

Jonathan had every reason to be jealous of David. After all, before David came along, Jonathan was a hero in his own right, and the king's son. But so great was Jonathan's love, that he deferred to David, rejoiced in his success, and encouraged him through his darkest times.

When Jonathan took off his robe, armor and even his sword and belt for David, he was symbolically giving David his friendship, his position, his very claim to the throne. He stripped himself of everything to give David his pledge of brotherly love.

Is this not the kind of love Jesus gave to us? He stripped Himself of His royal position and "made Himself of no reputation, taking the form of a servant, and coming in the likeness of men. And being found in appearance as a man, He humbled Himself and became obedient to the point of death, even the death of the cross" (Philippians 2:7-8).

In a very politically dangerous time, David learned the principle the apostle John taught centuries later: "There is no fear in love; but perfect love casts out fear, because fear involves torment. But he who fears has not been made perfect in love" (1 John 4:18). Saul tormented David, Jonathan loved him.

Saul's jealousy turned David away, causing Saul to lose one of his greatest allies and most faithful servants. Being driven away by the king he admired and served faithfully, discouraged David tremendously. But Jonathan, whose name means "gift of God," was truly a gift to David from the Lord.

David could have suspected Jonathan's motives, but so honest and trustworthy was Jonathan's friendship, that David knew he could trust him implicitly. Jonathan stood up to his own father, the king, and more than once saved David's life.

A Legacy of Loyalty

The impact of Jonathan's death on David is best understood by reading David's own words:

> *"How the mighty have fallen in the midst of the battle!*
>
> *I am distressed for you, my brother Jonathan;*
>
> *You have been very pleasant to me;*
>
> *Your love to me was wonderful..."*

> (2 Samuel 1:25-27)

David lost his best friend, but was left with a legacy of love and loyalty, which he could only have learned through a friend like Jonathan. After David ascended to the throne, he quickly became politically powerful and respected. No one would have been surprised if he ruthlessly wiped out any remnants of the house of Saul, after all he had suffered at the old king's hands. It was probably expected.

But David did not forget his loyal friend. When they were young, Jonathan pledged a covenant with the house of David. Now David would have a chance to return that loyalty.

To the surprise, I'm sure, of many, David went inquiring: "Is there still anyone who is left of the house of Saul, that I may show him kindness for Jonathan's sake?" (2 Samuel 1).

He found Mephibosheth, Jonathan's crippled son. In a poignant meeting, Mephibosheth bows down to David, hoping for mercy, only to have David restore to him all the lands of his father, as well as an honored place at David's table.

This was not typical behavior for a king of this era. But it was for David, a man who had learned loyalty through the love of a friend.

Jonathan foreshadowed the covenant of love Jesus made with us. His covenant with David made its indelible mark on the soul of this unique and godly king.

David would have many more people influence his life in the years to come, but I believe these three were used to prepare him to be king more than all the others; three people handpicked by God to build character in His chosen servant.

CHAPTER IV

LESSONS FROM THE CAVE

"In the shadow of Your wings I make my refuge."

Psalm 57

A Rising Star

David was a rising star. The people were singing his praises throughout the land. It seemed he could do no wrong. Look how he is described in chapter 18 of 1 Samuel:

"The women sang as they danced, 'Saul has slain his thousands, and David his ten thousands'" (v. 8).

"And David behaved wisely in all his ways, and the Lord was with him" v. 14).

"All of Israel and Judah loved David..." (v. 16).

"Now Michal, Saul's daughter, loved David" (v. 20).

"Then the princes of the Philistines went out to war. And so it was, whenever they went out, that David behaved more wisely than all the servants of Saul, so that his name became highly esteemed" (v. 30).

David was on a roll. He had the esteem of his peers, the nation, even the king's daughters. It would appear that nothing could stop him, especially with God's anointing so obviously upon him.

But the foundation of leadership has to be character, not charisma. Saul had charisma. David clearly had charisma. But God was looking for a man of *character* to be upon the throne of Israel, and He knew that David's character needed more development.

An Angry King

We went through chapter 18 and picked out the good things written about David. Now let's look through it again and see how Saul responded:

> *"Then Saul was very angry and the saying displeased him...so Saul eyed David from that day forward" (v. 8-9).*

> *"And Saul cast the spear [in his hand], for he said, 'I will pin David to the wall.' But David escaped..." (v. 11).*

> *"When Saul saw that he [David] behaved very wisely, he was afraid of him" (v. 15).*

> *"Saul thought to make David fall by the hand of the Philistines" (v. 25).*

> *"Thus Saul saw and knew that the Lord was with David, and that Michal, Saul's daughter, loved him; and Saul was still more afraid of David. So Saul became David's enemy continually" (v. 28-29).*

Saul's jealousy and bitterness were about to become David's torment. Jonathan clued David in on a plot to kill him, and thus began David's flight into the wilderness.

Dark Days

When David left to hide in the caves of Judea, he probably thought he'd be there a couple of weeks, just until things cooled down. I doubt that he and the band of men who eventually joined him ever thought they would be living this Robin Hood existence for over ten years!

A.W. Tozer wrote, "There are those times that before God uses a man or woman greatly, He will hurt them deeply."

Indeed, it was during these very dark and painful days that David wrote some of the most moving and passionate Psalms found in the Bible. I believe that it was during this time that his relationship with the Lord was deepened in a marvelous way. God drew David into an intimate relationship with Him and taught him some of the most important lessons of his life.

Compassion

Imagine for a moment that you're David. You've just barely escaped with your life from a mad king, and now you've found what you think will be a temporary refuge in a deserted desert cave. It's lonely and dark, but for now, you're safe.

That's the position David was in when he looked up one day and saw a few stragglers on the horizon. As their number grew, he began to recognize some of them, including his own brothers "and all his father's house" (1 Samuel 22).

Eventually four hundred men joined him. A small army! And what an army it was. Here's how they are described in the next verse: "Everyone who was in distress, everyone who was in debt, and everyone who was discontented gathered to him. So he became captain over them."

All the most discouraged, disenchanted, miserable and outcast people in the kingdom appeared to have rallied around him. And then there was his family, who wasn't in much better shape. After all, now that David was a known enemy of the king, his family was out of favor as well.

So Now What?

David understood loneliness. He had learned to be tender-hearted toward defenseless creatures. He was sensitive to the Lord's leading. Now he begins to exercise the lesson of compassion as he deals with all the people who have thrown themselves into his care.

First, his family. Remember, David's own father at one time did not hold David in high enough esteem to introduce him to Samuel. Even so, David honored his family by going to the king of Moab and pleading, "Please let my mother and father come here with you until I know what God will do for me" (1 Samuel 22:3).

Next, he must have looked over this motley crew of outcast and distressed men, and I think his shepherding instincts took over. He became their captain, and in turn, they became his loyal men.

He wasn't alone anymore, but I'm sure the situation must have appeared bleak as he studied his prospects. Besides fighting Saul, he also had to battle the enemies of despair, discouragement, fear and the loneliness of leadership.

No wonder David poured out his heart to the Lord in the Psalms he wrote from the caves. Look at Psalm 142:

Maschil of David; a prayer when he was in the cave.

I cry out to the Lord with my voice; with my voice to the Lord I make my supplication.

I pour out my complaint before Him; I declare before Him my trouble.

When my spirit was overwhelmed within me, then You knew my path. In the way in which I walk they have secretly set a snare for me.

Look on my right hand, and see,

For there is no one who acknowledges me;

Refuge has failed me;

No one cares for my soul.

I cried out to you, O LORD:

I said, You are my refuge,

My portion in the land of the living.

Attend to my cry;

For I am brought very low;

Deliver me from my persecutors; for they are stronger than I.

Bring my soul out of prison, that I may praise Your name:

The righteous shall surround me,

For You shall deal bountifully with me.

When David felt alone with his fear, when his spirit was overwhelmed, when his soul felt as if he was in prison, he knew where to turn. "You are my refuge!" he cried to the Lord. His heart yearned for God's protection, His comfort, His presence. David was being drawn deeper and deeper into a knowledge of the mercy and compassion of the Lord. The darker the caves, the more real the presence of the Lord became in David's life.

Failure. Fear. Defeat. Discouragement. Hopelessness. Betrayal. Sorrow. Pain. These fiery darts pierce our souls and the darkness of the caves threatens to imprison us. No wonder David groaned, "My spirit was overwhelmed"!

In those dark and secret caves, God etched into David's heart the deep, deep lesson of compassion, as only God can do.

With his heart resolutely fixed on the Lord, the lessons David learned would minister to others through his Psalms for generations to come.

The apostle Paul, who I'm sure drew comfort from David's Psalms during his own trials, wrote of his experiences, "Blessed be...the Father of mercies and the God of all comfort, who comforts us in our tribulation, that we may be able to comfort those who are in trouble, with the comfort with which we ourselves are comforted by God" (2 Cor. 1:4).

Never again would David look at another human being and not be able to have some understanding and compassion for his predicament.

God desired a leader who would treat the people of Israel as a family. David saw himself as a servant to his people, while Saul ruled the people and expected them to be his servants.

Hiding in dark caves, praying for the welfare of his family, and being responsible for the well-being of four hundred down-and-out men, gave David leadership capabilities and a compassionate heart which never would have come from living in the king's palace.

A final note: Eventually these four hundred men followed David to the palace and became known as "David's mighty men." What an example of God's mercy and grace!

Contemplation

Great leaders need to balance the time they spend in front of the people they are leading, with the time they spend alone with God.

The cave time taught David to be alone with God. Imagine how close he must have grown to the Lord during this time. How powerful God's presence must have been when he wrote such magnificent and moving praises to the Lord as Psalm 57:

Be merciful to me, O God, be merciful to me!

For my soul trusts in You;

And in the shadow of Your wings I make my refuge,

Until these calamities have passed by.

I will cry out to God Most High,

To God who performs all things for me.

He shall send from heaven and save me;

He reproaches the one who would swallow me up.

God shall send forth His mercy and His truth.

My soul is among lions;

I lie among the sons of men who are set on fire

Whose teeth are spears and arrows,

And their tongue a sharp sword.

Be exalted O God, above the heavens;

Let Your glory be above all the earth.

They have prepared a net for my steps;

My soul is bowed down;

They have dug a pit before me;

In the midst of it

they themselves have fallen.

My heart is steadfast [fixed], O God, my heart is steadfast ;

I will sing and give praise.

Awake my glory!

Awake, lute and harp!

I will awaken the dawn.

I will praise You, O Lord, among the peoples;

I will sing to You among the nations.

For Your mercy reaches unto the heavens,

And Your truth into the clouds.

Be exalted, O God, above the heavens;

Let Your glory be above all the earth.

When do we usually forget to pray? When everything is going fine. When do we begin to pray? When does prayer become a necessity in our lives like breathing or eating? When we're stuck in a dark cave, fearful and alone.

God had to carve this lesson into the heart of David, because though he went through this period of tribulation, the majority of David's life was going to be spent in a place of power and prestige. David was going to become such an important person, so wealthy and influential, that it was important for the *character of contemplation* to be instilled into him.

David needed to be taught the lesson that when life is good, when you're wealthy, powerful, successful—when you appear to have it all, you need to pray just as fervently as you do when you are in the caves.

God allows us cave times so that our characters are built on a foundation of prayer, not of self-reliance. C.H. Spurgeon wisely said, "Had David prayed as much in his palace as he did in his cave, he might never have fallen into the act which brought such misery upon his latter days."

Cheerfulness and Joy

David learned the joy of the Lord in the caves. Can you imagine? How true it is that God's ways are not our ways! Who among us would have chosen to teach someone to be cheerful, positive, encouraging and full of joy by sticking them in a dark cave?

But God wanted David to learn a lesson so vital that it would shape his future as king and of the nation of Israel. 'David,' God was saying, 'if you can experience the joy of My presence, and if you can maintain a cheerful countenance which radiates that joy, even in the darkness of the caves, then you can experience My joy anywhere.' You cannot be defeated. You cannot be discouraged, if you remember this lesson.

The third Psalm, we know with certainty, David wrote from the caves is Psalm 34. Look at how he expresses the joy of the Lord, even in his troubles:

> *I will bless the LORD at all times: His praise shall continually be in my mouth.*

> *My soul shall make its boast in the Lord: the humble shall hear of it, and be glad.*

> *O magnify the Lord with me, and let us exalt his name together.*

I sought the Lord, and He heard me, and delivered me from all my fears...

O taste and see that the Lord is good: blessed is the man who trusts in Him...

The Lord is near to those who have a broken heart; and saves such as have a contrite spirit.

Many are the afflictions of the righteous: but the Lord delivers him out of them all.

The Lord redeems the soul of His servants: and none of those who trust in Him shall be condemned.

"The joy of the Lord is your strength," the Bible tells us (Nehemiah 8:10). If that isn't true in your life, then you are lacking an essential element of your Christian walk. Lack of joy is a major character flaw!

Jesus said, "You are the light of the world." You may never be a king or even a leader in the traditional sense of the word. But Jesus is telling us that we are the living Gospel, the only exposure some people ever have to the Good News. If people who never attend church or hear a sermon were simply watching the pages of your life, would they read there the love of God, the mercy of God, the joy of the Lord? If they read just your life, would they see enough character to reflect the love of Jesus Christ?

David was a cheerful person. Even out in the caves he could cry out exultantly, "O magnify the Lord with me! Let us exalt His name together!"

He was learning what God wanted him to learn: that joy is not dependent upon circumstances. Happiness comes and goes, but JOY—the joy of the Lord is internal and eternal. The kind of JOY which God will impress into our characters is everlasting, bountiful, strength-giving and enables us to radiate cheerfulness, even in the darkest of times.

During those years spent in the caves, David was transformed by the Lord from an innocent shepherd boy to a rugged and righteous man of God. He was now a man of integrity and honor, a man after God's own heart. He was almost ready to be king.

CHAPTER V

HALFTIME

"Search me, O God, and know my heart"
(Psalm 139:23).

One Step From Eternity

Death had been chasing at David's heels for several years now. Its threat had become his constant companion. We can see it in the Psalms he wrote, and we can read it in the continuing story of his adventures in exile.

"There is but a step between me and death," he confided to Jonathan on one of the many occasions he was escaping Saul's traps.

After another encounter with Saul, David spoke to himself with resignation, *"Now I shall perish someday at the hand of Saul"* (1 Samuel 27:1). His years of running had left him weary. Some of his youthful invincibility was wearing thin. He had reached a stage in life which we all have to deal with sooner or later–acknowledging the reality of death.

This stage begins not only when we face our own mortality, but with the passing of people close to us. The deep lessons the Lord etches into our hearts through this often difficult and painful stage of life, will prove to be some of the strongest building blocks in the formation of our characters.

While David was in the midst of his battles with Saul, Samuel the prophet died (1 Samuel 25:1). Ironically, the prophet to whom the nation would not listen when they demanded a king, was now lamented throughout the land. We don't know much from the Scriptures regarding the personal relationship between David and Samuel, but as the prophet who anointed David king and spoke to the nation on behalf of the Lord, Samuel's influence was surely felt.

For David, Samuel was like many of the older people in my life; I depend on their wisdom and their presence. Just knowing they are *there* is reassuring. Samuel's death undoubtedly left a great void in David's life.

Soon after Samuel's death, David's struggles with Saul came to an end—but at a great price.

"Saul, his three sons, his armor-bearer and all his men died together the same day...they found Saul and his three sons fallen on Mount Gilboa" (1 Samuel 31:6,8). Those sons included Jonathan.

When news of their deaths reached David, his grief was felt throughout the land. He and his men mourned and wept and fasted for Jonathan and Saul. After hearing the details of their deaths, David poured his sorrow into a song, as he often did. This one, he commanded his people "to teach the children of Judah":

"The beauty of Israel is slain in high places!

How the mighty have fallen!

O mountains of Gilboa,

Let there be no dew, nor let there be rain upon you,

Nor fields of offering.

For the shield of the mighty is defiled there...

Saul and Jonathan were beloved and pleasant in their lives,

And in their death they were not divided...

I am distressed for you, my brother Jonathan;

You have been very pleasant to me;

Your love was wonderful..."

Those who have lost someone dearly loved, can understand the grief that David experienced. Even Saul, David's enemy, was a loss, for all he had been in David's life. But Jonathan—Jonathan was like losing a beloved brother, something I can understand personally.

My brother Glenn, who was just a year younger than me, was hit by a car and killed when he was 36 years old. His death was a shock to me and my family.

Even though I have conducted many funerals and counseled many others through this sorrow, not since the death of our infant son, have I been forced to face death in such a personal way. Losing Glenn hurt our family greatly. We miss him. We mourn for what he never experienced, for the times he won't be with us to laugh, to talk, to just enjoy one another's company. There is an irreconcilable void at our family gatherings. I grieve for my parents, for having lost a son, for myself for having lost a brother, for my other brother Greg, who was Glenn's twin.

Waves of grief come and go, and can't be escaped. Knowing that Glenn is with the Lord brings immeasurable comfort. But when the waves hit, I understand the cries of the psalmist: "...all your waves and breakers have swept over me" (Psalm 42:7). Death takes us through deep waters and dark, shadowy valleys. Death is a thief and a robber. It takes from us the very thing God bestowed upon us—life. It is a reality. There is no getting around the tragedy that is death.

The moment for facing eternity had come to David. His own death. The prophet's death. His enemy's death. His beloved friend. He had much to contemplate and reflect upon.

Success to Significance

In his book, *Why Grace Changes Everything*, Pastor Chuck Smith writes, "God has a special work for each of us to do and it is necessary that all of us be prepared for that work. Many of us will spend the majority of our lives in preparation before our day will come...

"Wherever we find ourselves, God has a reason for placing us there. He has His hand upon our lives and upon each circumstance in our lives. We may be going through difficult trials, but hardships are necessary. God wants to develop in us the characteristics that will enable us to fulfill His plan for us."

David's destiny was to be king of Israel. Everything that had happened to him up to this point, was preparation.

The deaths of three influential people marked a significant impasse in David's life. With Saul's death, he was about to be recognized as the king. Though he would be ruling over a divided kingdom at first, it was the beginning of the fulfillment of David's destiny.

Let's stop for a moment and think about David's life and relate it to our own.

David was no longer a kid. He had passed through adolescence and early manhood, weathered the trials, and had matured into a man God could use. He was now probably in his thirties. By the time he finished fighting the wars that would unite his kingdom, he would be close to forty. A very typical age for a man or woman to stop and reflect upon the direction and meaning of life.

We can tell from the Psalms David wrote during his lulls between battles and his lonely nights in the caves, that reflecting and contemplating were indeed what he was doing.

David had reached what Bob Buford calls *Halftime* in his book by that name. "Recently I have begun looking at my own life through the metaphor of a football game," he writes. "Up until my thirty-fifth year, I was in the first half. Then, circumstances intervened that sent me into halftime."

Like many men in our society, David's first half was actually somewhat typical, if not in actual details, at least in the lessons learned. We spend the first halves of our lives getting educated, trained, or somehow prepared for our work. Some go to college, some learn in the field (like David, literally). We usually find a wife and start a family (David had married more than once by now), achieve some successes, suffer a few setbacks, and gain some sort of professional reputation.

It's not easy getting to halftime, as many of us, including David, discover. Most of us take some hard hits and suffer through some painful injuries.

But if the pain is part of the preparation, then now is the time for stopping to think about where you are going and what the rest of your life will mean. I like the way Bob Buford puts it: *"If the first half of the journey was a quest for success, the second half is a journey to significance."*

The significance of the second half of David's life would lie in his relationship with the Lord. Everything that had happened to him up to this point was preparation and progress towards David's position as king. Everything was part of a divine plan.

The greatness of David is found in his desire to fulfill God's plan for his life, and his ability to be satisfied with whatever God had for him. For all of us, whether we are called to be a king or a courtyard servant, in whatever position we find ourselves, if we are asking God to fulfill *His* purposes in our lives, we will be satisfied. There, in the will of the Lord, will be satisfaction, service and significance.

David understood this principle when he wrote:

> *"Blessed is the man whom You choose, and cause to approach You, that he may dwell in Your courts. We shall be satisfied with the goodness of Your house."*

(Psalm 65)

The question we all need to stop and ask ourselves is, are we fulfilling God's plan for our lives? And if not, we need to ask the Lord, just as David did many, many times, to order our steps and reveal His plan. The very first thing David did after lamenting the deaths of Jonathan and Saul was to ask the Lord what his next action should be (2 Samuel 2:1).

"Teach me Your ways," he implored in Psalm 27. "You are my God. My times are in Your hands..." (Psalm 31:14,15). Always, David turned to the Lord for His strength, His help, His direction.

The significance of David's life was completely rooted in his relationship and reliance upon the Lord. "My voice You shall hear in the morning," he promised the Lord. Daily, he sought the Lord's will for his life, and daily, I believe God guided and directed the way David should go.

Any significance we hope to achieve must be based on God's Word and will for our lives. Everything else is sinking sand, as the song goes.

As exciting and thrilling as the first half might be, we all know that games are won or lost in the second half. David was about to enter the second half of his life. God had taught him many lessons. But there was an especially important one that David needed to learn to finish well.

A Foundation of Grace

The apostle Paul wrote of his calling into God's service, "When God, who set me apart from birth and called me by His grace, was pleased to reveal His Son in me so that I might preach Him among the Gentiles, I did not consult any man..." (Galatians 1:15, NIV).

The key phrase here is *called me by His grace*. In the years to come, David would encounter the many challenges of ruling a kingdom, not the least being his own weakness in the face of temptation.

To understand the secret of David's greatness, we have to go back to that key phrase: called by His grace. Because David was called by the grace of God, and because he knew it—he knew that "he who trusts in the Lord, mercy shall surround him" (Psalm 32)— David, I believe, knew that he could be nothing greater than God allowed him to be.

At the "halftime" of his life, David learned the most important lesson of all—that every hour, with every breath and heartbeat, he needed to live *solely* by the grace of God.

He was going to need a great measure of that grace in the years to come. Halftime was over.

CHAPTER VI

NO COMPROMISE

"If we are faithless, He remains faithful..."

2 Timothy 2:13

David's Epitaph

"You have been foolish," the old prophet thundered to Saul. "Your kingdom shall not continue. The Lord has sought for Himself a man after His own heart."

In that phrase, David's epitaph was written. When the life of David is taught, discussed, dramatized or otherwise portrayed, he is inevitably described as "the man after God's own heart."

After the deaths of Saul and Jonathan, David's ascension to the throne marked the beginning of years of triumphs and a rise in stature for the nation of Israel. David transformed Israel from a weak and divided kingdom into a formidable empire. The life of David continued on its legendary course as his reputation as a warrior, poet, king, friend and spiritual leader spiraled upward.

When I think of David in those lofty, historic terms, he almost loses me. I can relate to the young shepherd boy who was given a commission for which he was totally unqualified. I can relate to the young man hiding in the caves, battling fear and loneliness. I can relate to the man who grieved over the loss of loved ones and was forced to face the reality of death. I can relate to the necessary maturing process of stopping to evaluate and take stock of one's life.

But I'll never be the heroic king, renaissance man and statesman that David ultimately became.

That's when I have to remember, that when God called David a man after "His own heart," it wasn't because of David's accomplishments. *It was because of what God did in and through David.*

Next to Jesus, David is given more space in the Bible than any other person. David is a role model for us to learn how God works in our lives from beginning to end. And, the last years of David's life were certainly no less dramatic or character forming than the early years.

Restoring a Compromised Nation

The nation of Israel in David's time was in reality a huge, extended family, made up of twelve tribes, all related to each other. Like many such families, they squabbled and fought amongst themselves, with painful results.

With David ready to take his anointed position as king, the family feud heated up. A faction of the nation wanted Saul's son to succeed to the throne. In spite of every indication that David was God's choice, for seven-and-a-half long years the rebellious faction chose to hang onto the forsaken house of Saul, and the nation was plunged into a bloody and hateful civil war. Years of battles, death, diminished prosperity and personal losses followed.

They were victorious, yet painful years for David. Men he admired fell in battle. Though he fought for a righteous cause, the cost was great.

In this instance, we have to step away from David the man for a moment and look at him as a symbol.

Besides being a role model, David is also used in Scripture as a type of Jesus Christ. The nation of Israel is like the Body of Christ—our Christian family. The house of Saul represents the kingdom of the flesh and the world. The house of David represents the kingdom of God. When the rightful king rules, there is harmony and prosperity in the nation and in the family. When part of the family rebels, or when the wrong king is on the throne, civil war within the family, the nation and the individual tears apart our lives.

As I imagine this whole scene being played out, watching David trying to unite his kingdom, I realize that we are being challenged as individuals and as the Church of Jesus Christ: Who will you serve? Which king will you follow? Are you compromising your faith and your life? Do you understand the consequences of compromise?

Just as the children of Israel watched their families and children suffer in the heat of civil war, so we see our families and children pay for our compromise and hypocrisy. Hypocrisy may seem like a harsh word, but how else do you think it looks to our children when we preach and say one thing at church and live another way at home or at work or out in the world?

How can we expect our children to live uncompromised lives, to remain pure during their growing up years; how can we demand of them that they not drink and take drugs; how can we expect them to live dedicated, committed lives for the Lord, if they don't see it in us?

Just as the nation of Israel had to choose the house of David over the house of Saul, so we are being asked to make a choice between two warring factions: the Lordship of Christ or the compromising, weak life that Satan wants to inflict upon us.

"I never knew you..."

One of the most powerful and fearful Scriptures in the Bible for me is Matthew 7:21-23. Jesus is explaining that "Not everyone who says to Me, 'Lord, Lord,' shall enter the kingdom of heaven, but he who does the will of my Father in heaven." Many will come to Him saying, "Lord, have we not prophesied in Your name and done many wonders in Your name?" And because they chose not to follow Him, not to live for Him, all those good deeds and signs and wonders counted for nothing. In the day of judgment, Jesus will turn to them and declare, "I never knew you; depart from Me, you who practice lawlessness!"

Whew! That Scripture strikes conviction in my heart. "Let each man examine himself," the apostle Paul admonished. We need to stop and take an honest look at our lives. If our allegiance is confused, and the resulting turmoil in our lives is proof of that confusion, then we need to stop the civil war and come back to that place of peace, reconciliation and unity with our Lord and our brothers and sisters in Christ.

Being at war is tiring and painful. But it is the bone-weariness, total exhaustion and end-of-the-line despair that causes us to desire the will of God. The aching bondage of sin must often be felt before we crave the freedom and liberty of Christ.

Sometimes prodigal children have to live in the wretchedness of a far country before they can recognize the blessings, comfort and love of home. The children of Israel in Moses' day, groaned in slavery for 400 years under Pharaoh's rule before they had the courage to flee for the Promised Land and God's ways.

It took the nation of Israel over seven years of bloody, civil war to realize that it was time to surrender to the rightful king. ***Peace required a change of masters.***

How to Return to the Kingdom of God

David's hard fought war to unite the kingdom finally ended. David won the hearts of his people by being consistently just and generous toward his friends and enemies alike. The anointing of the Lord upon his life was growing more and more evident to the people.

The same war goes on in our individual lives as well. A war between two natures, a war between the kingdom of darkness and the kingdom of light. A hard fought battle wages over our souls and eternal destinies, and when we compromise, we end up much like Israel: Divided, confused and hurting.

The steps toward healing a compromised life are clearly laid out in 2 Samuel 5:1 and 2.

In verse one, the people came to David and said, "Indeed, we are your bone and your flesh." They surrendered because they finally recognized their true family. We are related by blood, they said. We belong together.

The people of Israel humbled themselves before David, appealing to him for mercy on the basis of their kinship. Likewise, God asks us to **recognize our true family**. We no longer belong to the world. We are born into God's family. We are related by the blood of Christ, united in His Spirit. "He who is joined to the Lord is one spirit with Him," Paul wrote (1 Corinthians 6:17). When we are joined together by Christ, we are one with Him—and each other!

Secondly, the people of Israel admitted their past failures. "Also, in times past, when Saul was king over us..." They confessed, we followed the wrong master, we went the wrong way.

We also need to **confess our sins** to the Lord. We need to admit, *I compromised. I gave in to worldliness, to the weakness of the flesh.*

Once you have confessed, you must believe what God's Word says, that "He is faithful and just to forgive us our sins and to cleanse us from all unrighteousness" (1 John 1:9). He forgives and He forgets, and so must you.

Paul declared in Philippians 3:13: "...one thing I do, forgetting those things which are behind and reaching forward to those things which are ahead..." **Let go of the past**, God says. Move ahead. Confess, repent, then take God's forgiveness and go forward.

Finally, the children of Israel acknowledged to David, "...you were the one who led Israel out and brought them in; and the Lord said to you, 'You shall shepherd my people and be ruler over Israel' " (verse 2).

They recognized God's grace. They now understood that all along, even while they were submitted to the house of Saul, by the grace of God, they did not lose their kingdom.

We need to **recognize the grace of God** in our lives as well. How often we unfaithfully compromise our lives, only to experience God's graciousness toward us. He never forsakes us. According to Scripture, it's not in His character to do so. "If we are faithless, He remains faithful; He cannot deny Himself" (2 Timothy 2:13).

The very character of God, the character He formed in David, and the character He is building in each of His children is a reflection of His amazing grace.

CHAPTER VII

A MAN AFTER GOD'S OWN HEART

"Create in me a clean heart, O God..."

Psalm 51

Of all the stories in the Bible related to David, surely the two which are the most famous are the accounts of David and Goliath and of David and Bathsheba.

In one, he slays a giant. In the other, he falls to an even greater enemy, his own lust.

Paradoxically, it is the story of David's sin with Bathsheba which reveals his true greatness. Through this timeless drama, we learn why God called David "a man after His own heart."

A Disappointing Setback

The kingdom was united under the rightful king, and David's reign was a success. More than a success. He had also achieved the significance we discussed in the previous chapter. He triumphantly brought the Ark of the Covenant to Jerusalem, thereby fulfilling His deep desire to restore the nation as a center of worship to the Lord.

Now, with his nation at peace, David wanted to continue to honor the Lord. He went to Nathan the prophet with a proposal to build a temple for the Lord. Even Nathan was excited about the project—until the Lord said *No*.

It was a major setback for David. Besides the fact that he thought he was doing something good for God, it would also be a real coup to be the one to build the Temple of the Lord!

Again, a test of character. How would David respond to being denied something he so passionately desired? Though he was deeply disappointed, David submitted to God's will and gratefully worshiped the Lord for all He had done for him already.

Everything from there on out is a chronicle of David's victories and the prosperity of his kingdom—until he did what so many of us do right in the midst of God's blessings. Succumb to the weakness of our flesh.

Sin

It was spring time, and according to 2 Samuel 11, "the time when kings go out to battle." Israel's armies were busy defending the nation, but David, this spring, "tarried at Jerusalem."

This was not typical of David. When his armies were fighting, and the kings were at war, David was usually with his men. Whether he was tired or preoccupied with something at home, for some reason, he had retreated from the battle.

One evening, David strolled along the roof of his palace. When he looked across the flat roof tops that are typical of Israeli architecture, he saw, in full view, a woman named Bathsheba bathing, "and the woman was very beautiful to behold."

Billy Graham has said that it is not the first look that gets us into trouble. It's that second and third one! In David's case, a glance turned into a gaze; that second look turned into lust.

He sent for Bathsheba, had intimate relations with her, and she became pregnant.

Kings did things like that in those days, even ones as noble as David. But this woman was the only wife of one of his most loyal soldiers, Uriah. David knew he had done something terribly wrong. In an effort to cover his sin, David brought Uriah home, flattered him with gifts, and encouraged him to go home and spend time with his wife.

But being the noble soldier that he was, Uriah did not sleep with Bathsheba, protesting that all the other soldiers "are encamped in the open field. Shall I then go to my house to eat and drink and to lie with my wife? I will not!"

David was busted. Now how will Bathsheba explain her pregnancy?

It's strange how one unconfessed sin begets another. David felt he had to get rid of Uriah, so he contrived a plot to have him sent into the heat of battle, where he was killed.

David is now guilty of adultery and murder. A man after God's own heart, guilty of two heinous crimes—and attempting to cover them up.

Nathan, the bravest man in the kingdom

If you can't relate to David the renaissance-type man and king, then can you relate to David the sinner?

Well, you say, I've never gone quite so far as to commit murder! The details of your life may differ, but in principle, David was like many of us. God had given him everything. He was a blessed man. But it was apparently not enough. The lust of the flesh is a powerful lure, and when we allow ourselves to be in a position to succumb, we fall, just as David did.

David married Bathsheba, and she gave birth to a son. What a constant reminder of his sin that child must have been!

A year passed. What a year for David that must have been; unreconciled sin and the memory of Uriah haunting his conscience. Finally the king's counselor, Nathan the prophet, was sent to David by the Lord. Nathan told David the story of a poor man with one little beloved lamb, who was taken advantage of by a rich, powerful land owner. The rich man, with hundreds of lambs and herds of his own, took the poor man's only lamb, and killed it for a meal.

David's anger exploded when he heard Nathan's report! The injustice of it! "As the Lord lives, the man who has done this shall surely die!" he declared. "And he shall restore fourfold for the lamb!" (2 Samuel 12:5,6).

David the law enforcer, champion of the underdog! His anger boiled out of him, uncharacteristically vengeful and bitter.

David was riddled with guilt. His flash of anger at Nathan's report could easily have been due to his own pangs of conscience. Just like those little warning lights that flash on our car dashboards to warn us of impending trouble, so turmoil, anger and depression are warning signs of issues that are unresolved in our lives.

We can choose to pay attention to those little lights—idiot lights they're called—pull over to the side of the road, stop for a moment and assess what's wrong. Or, we can ignore them until our engine blows up. If we're really out of control, we can just take a hammer and smash them.

I think David was about to blow up.

That's when Nathan, who I think must have been a very brave man, looked David straight in the face, and said, "You are the man!"

David must have felt as if he'd been struck. As Nathan unrelentingly recounted his sin, David fell deeper and deeper under the conviction of the Holy Spirit. Judgment was pronounced. "...the sword shall never depart from your house...the child who was born to you shall surely die." The pain, the sorrow. David was guilty of inflicting so much on everyone around him.

Confession Time

But his response to the condemnation of sin is once again a role model for men and women everywhere: "I have sinned against the Lord."

No excuses. No pointing fingers at someone else. David immediately confesses, acquiesces, repents. *I am guilty! I have sinned against the Lord!* After his earlier outburst at Nathan's story, David knew he deserved to die.

Nathan's response from the Lord was also immediate: "The Lord has also put away your sin; you shall not die" (2 Samuel 12:13).

Do you realize the importance of that scenario? When pushed up against the wall, David had the power to deny Nathan's rebuke, even to have the prophet killed. But David humbled himself immediately before the Lord, and repented of his sin. He accepted the consequences of his actions, with humility. David understood that sin exacts a high price.

But he also knew he was forgiven! The Lord was ready to "put away" his sin! This was not a burden he would have to carry forever!

This is the lesson of David's life which we need to grasp. No matter how mighty, how blessed, how accomplished, how powerful, rich or famous he was, he was capable of sin—big time sin.

No man is above it. Not one of us. "All have sinned and fall short of the glory of God." *But no sin is so great that the grace of God is not greater still!*

The origin of the meaning of the word *forgive* is to untie a knot. How do you think David felt when at last his sin was out in the open and confessed? There was no more hiding, covering up, or wondering who would figure out what happened. He must have felt as if a thousand knots had been untied. The sense of relief was tremendous.

Who wants to go through life tied up in spiritual, emotional and mental knots? It's not healthy!

"If we confess our sins, He is faithful and just to forgive us our sins and to cleanse us from all unrighteousness" (I John 1:9). Forgiven and cleansed, with all the knots untied—now that's the way to live.

Grace

The Lord continued to build and develop David's character, throughout his life, just as He does with all of us. "For we are His workmanship, created in Christ Jesus for good works, which God prepared beforehand that we should walk in them" (Ephesians 2:10). The trials of his household, which grew in part out of his sin with Bathsheba, were a source of heartache for him.

Yet, even in what may have been his greatest disappointment—not being able to build the Temple—God taught him grace and used him as an example for generations to come.

When the Lord said *No* to David regarding the Temple, He also made him a promise: "When your days are fulfilled and you rest with your fathers, I will set up your seed after you, who will come from your body, and I will establish his kingdom.

"He shall build a house for My name and I will establish the throne of his kingdom forever" (2 Samuel 7:12-13).

In the long view, the Lord was referring to the fact that Jesus the Christ, the Messiah, the Holy One, would come through the line of David. Out of David's lineage, the Kingdom of God would be established forever.

In the immediate situation, the next chosen king over Israel, the one who would build the

Temple and take Israel into her Golden Age, was David's son, Solomon, the son of Bathsheba.

I doubt that the son of the woman with whom the king committed adultery would have been a lot of church committee's first choice. After all, what kind of example would that be for the kids?

God chose Solomon, because He was making a statement. God redeems sinners and makes them sons. He does this by forming the character in us of His own Son.

Choosing Solomon was God's way of pouring out unlimited grace upon his servant and of proving for all time that all things truly do work together for good "to those who love God, those who are called according to His purpose" (Romans 8:28).

And if ever there was a man who loved God and was called for a purpose, it was David.

Character

"to tear, cut in, engrave, cut into furrows."

Throughout David's life, the Lord allowed him to go through the tearing, cutting and engraving process. Only a man who has had God's character engraved deep into his soul could have written these words which so beautifully express the heart of a child of God:

The Lord is my shepherd;

I shall not want.

He makes me lie down in green pastures;

He leads me beside still waters.

He restores my soul;

He leads me in the paths of righteousness

For His name's sake.

Yea, though I walk through the valley of the shadow of death,

I will fear no evil;

For You are with me;

Your rod and Your staff, they comfort me.

You prepare a table before me in the presence of my enemies;

You anoint my head with oil;

My cup runs over.

Surely goodness and mercy

shall follow me

All the days of my life;

And I will dwell in the house

of the Lord forever.

Psalm 23

In closing...

"So he died in a good old age, full of riches and honor; and Solomon his son reigned in his place"

(1 Chronicles 29:28).

In the annals of world history, David emerges as one of civilization's most colorful and beloved figures. David is always remembered as a great king, statesman, warrior and poet. His heroic deeds, his character and charisma, his talent and his passion continue to be recounted, dramatized and studied.

But I believe that if David had a choice, he would ask us to look at his life as an example of God's handiwork. Of how the Lord can take any one of us, and regardless of our origins, our circumstances, our abilities, our strengths or our weaknesses—make us into a man or woman who will be remembered, like David, as someone "after God's own heart."

How to Become a Christian

First of all you must recognize that you are a sinner. Realize that you have missed the mark. This is true of each of us. We have deliberately crossed the line not once, but many times. The Bible says, *"All have sinned and fallen short of the glory of God"* (Romans 3:23). This is a hard admission for many to make, but if we are not willing to hear the bad news, we cannot appreciate and respond to the *good news*.

Second, we must realize that Jesus Christ died on the cross for us. Because of sin, God had to take drastic measures to reach us. So He came to this earth and walked here as a man. But Jesus was more than just a good man. He was the God-man—God incarnate—and that is why His death on the cross is so significant.

At the cross, God Himself—in the person of Jesus Christ—took our place and bore our sins. He paid for them and purchased our redemption.

Third, we must repent of our sin. God has commanded men everywhere to repent. Acts 3:19 states, *"Repent therefore and be converted, that your sins may be blotted out, so that times of refreshing may come from the presence of the Lord."* What does this word *repent* mean? It means to change direction–to hang a U-turn on the road of life. It means to stop living the kind of life we led previously and start living the kind of life outlined in the pages of the Bible. Now we must change and be willing to make a break with the past.

Fourth, we must receive Jesus Christ into our hearts and lives. Being a Christian is having God Himself take residence in our lives. John 1:12 tells us, *"But as many as received Him, to them He gave the right to become children of God."* We must receive Him. Jesus said, *"Behold, I stand at the door and knock. If anyone hears My voice and opens the door, I will come in…"* (Revelation 3:20). Each one of us must individually decide to open the door. How do we open it? Through prayer.

If you have never asked Jesus Christ to come into your life, you can do it right now. Here is a suggested prayer you might even pray.

Lord Jesus, I know that I am a sinner and I am sorry for my sin. I turn and repent of my sins right now. Thank You for dying on the cross for me and paying the price for my sin. Please come into my heart and life right now. Fill me with Your Holy Spirit and help me to be Your disciple. Thank You for forgiving me and coming into my life. Thank You that I am now a child of Yours and that I am going to heaven. In Jesus' name, I pray. Amen.

When you pray that prayer God will respond. You have made the right decision–the decision that will impact how you spend eternity. Now you will go to heaven, and in the meantime, find peace and the answers to your spiritual questions.

Taken from: *Life. Any Questions?*
by Greg Laurie, Copyright © 1995. Used by permission.

Other books available in this series...

Spiritual Warfare
by Brian Brodersen
Pastor Brian Brodersen of Calvary Chapel Costa Mesa, California, brings biblical balance and practical insight to the subject of spiritual warfare. 73 pages

The Psychologizing of the Faith
by Bob Hoekstra
Pastor Bob Hoekstra of Living in Christ Ministries calls the church to leave the broken cisterns of human wisdom, and to return to the fountain of living water flowing from our wonderful counselor, Jesus Christ. 74 pages.

Effective Prayer Life
by Chuck Smith
Pastor Chuck Smith of Calvary Chapel Costa Mesa, California, discusses the principles of prayer, the keys to having a dynamic prayer life, and the victorious results of such a life. It will stir in your heart a desire to "pray without ceasing." 120 pages.

Practical Christian Living
by Wayne Taylor
Pastor Wayne Taylor of Calvary Fellowship in Seattle, Washington, takes us through a study of Romans 12 and 13 showing us what practical Christian living is all about. 164 pages.

Worship and Music Ministry
by Rick Ryan & Dave Newton
Pastor Rick Ryan and Dave Newton of Calvary Chapel Santa Barbara, California, give us solid biblical insight into the important subjects of worship and music ministry within the body of Christ. 90 pages.

Overcoming Sin & Enjoying God
by Danny Bond
Pastor Danny Bond of Pacific Hills Church in Aliso Viejo, California, shows us, through practical principles, how it's possible to live in victory over sin and have constant fellowship with our loving God. 90 pages.

Answers for the Skeptic
by Scott Richards
Pastor Scott Richards of Calvary Fellowship in Tucson, Arizona, shows us what to say when our faith is challenged, and how to answer the skeptic in a way that opens hearts to the love and truth of Jesus Christ. 55 pages.

The Afterglow
by Henry Gainey
Pastor Henry Gainey of Calvary Chapel Thomasville, Georgia, gives instruction in conducting and understanding the proper use of the gifts of the Holy Spirit in an "Afterglow Service." 150 pages.

Final Curtain
by Chuck Smith
Pastor Chuck Smith of Calvary Chapel Costa Mesa, California, provides insight into God's prophetic plan and shows how current events are leading to the time when one climactic battle will usher in eternity. 96 pages.

Creation by Design
by Mark Eastman, M.D.
Mark Eastman, M.D., of Genesis Outreach in Temecula, California, carefully examines and clarifies the evidence for a Creator God, as he shows the reader the amazing hand of design in creation. 62 pages.

For ordering information, please contact:
The Word For Today
P.O. Box 8000, Costa Mesa, CA 92628
(800) 272-WORD
Also, visit us on the Internet at:
www.twft.com